Cover art by   Reverend Albert Wagner
From the private collection of   Thomas Sayers Ellis

Author photo by   Julie Philips

Published in the United States by   Fence Books
                                           New Library 320
                                           University at Albany
                                           1400 Washington Avenue
                                           Albany, NY 12222
                                           www.fencebooks.com

Book design by   Rebecca Wolff

Fence Books are distributed by   University Press of New England
                                           www.upne.com

and printed in Canada by   Westcan Printing Group
                                           www.westcanpg.com

Library of Congress Cataloguing in Publication Data
        Sharma, Prageeta [1972–]
        Infamous Landscapes/ Prageeta Sharma

Library of Congress Control Number: 2007933972

ISBN 1-934200-08-5
ISBN 13: 978-1-934200-08-7

first edition

 ARE PUBLISHED IN PARTNERSHIP WITH

AND

AND WITH HELP FROM

State of the Arts

NYSCA

THIS BOOK IS MADE POSSIBLE IN PART BY A GENEROUS FACE OUT GRANT FROM

COUNCIL OF LITERARY MAGAZINES & PRESSES
w w w . c l m p . o r g

IN PARTNERSHIP WITH THE JEROME FOUNDATION

INFAMOUS LANDSCAPES

prageeta sharma

ALBANY, NEW YORK

INFAMOUS LANDSCAPES

ACKNOWLEDGMENTS

Thank you to the editors of the following journals, periodicals, anthologies, and installations, for printing these poems (in various forms & versions):

Boston Review, Canwehaveourballback.com, Contemporary Voices from the Eastern World: An Anthology of Poems (W. W. Norton, fall 2007), *Combo, Encyclopedia: Volume I, The East Village.com, The Hat, The Indiana Review, Interlope, Jubilat, Le Petite Zine, Lit, The Literary Review, Kundiman/Verlaine* Series, and *Vanitas.*

I am grateful also to the following family, friends, and colleagues:

The Sharma family, Aja Sherrard, Donna and John Shafer, Vera Fraschetti, Rebecca Wolff, Thomas Sayers Ellis, Joanna Klink, Katherine Lederer, C. D. Wright, Forrest Gander, Karen Volkman, Nina D'Amario, Caroline Crumpacker, Rahna Reiko Rizzuto, Paul Violi, David Lehman, Major Jackson, the Council of Literary Magazines and Presses, Cambridge College, University of Montana, Goddard College, The New School, The Poetry Society of America, The Millay Colony, and the many students and teachers over the years who have provided time, warmth, and engaging dialogue. Thank you to Dale for unending support.

This work is indebted to my readings of the works of George Oppen, William Wordsworth, and Barbara Guest.

CONTENTS

i. clouds & things

ii. be my foreground

TO MY MOTHER AND FATHER

i. clouds & things

CANDOR

Candor may have indeed arrived,
after years of mistrust,
persisting on my part,
as to what exactly it is.

Above the water, I have loved so much
that it is unbearable to divulge

any method of explanation that's unmediated.
Of candor in the grass,
feelings can disqualify future feelings.
It's the sun now, or it's the landscape
or the jaunts in the park.
I had wanted more and was slapped in the face.
So here I am, in response to excess,
a juvenile high on Marxism,
a false and reconstructed
humanist, and even if Marxism is passé,

I lasted this long on other misguided ideas.
Onward to careless valentines, situational and loveless
hysteria, mismatched enthusiasm with a bare ankle entwined.

Moreover, whatever passes by, whatever we jerk our bodies for,
collapsing down from the branches,
we look up, here, a modern tree, blustering, agile, and ambitious.

WORRIES AJAR

In a tank, a small cistern in the body
was where the grief overtook me.
Perhaps angst. Because my gold coin didn't feel real enough,
I just burned and wandered.
The guild, the employer, the king, the staff,
made gentle guidelines, nudged outright but retracted the gesture,
and even when silent treatments were administered,
they became light sentences.
Nothing was truly ham-handed; I was not having bad luck.
My pain was dull, my house was plentiful.
My dress was spun with care; I had been reminded that it was.
My fishbowl was husky and that's what I told myself, no more
Indigo, no more indigent fantasies. I have not swam in jilted
dreams nor breached a belt of coldness so low.

ESCAPE

I had triumphed in bringing my life out of its
irreparable smallness where it had been close to being extinguished
or deactivated. It was a plain problem; it was the curse of the malcontent monster
who casually controlled my activity—
soothing me with sooty dishrags, cold cuts, the domesticated bleat—
the sunshine dank without luminous intervals.
New York was an icy dew of Neanderthal meets Oppenheimer.
People fussy with judgment and fuzzy with fabric.
In which case, I had to remove contracts from view politely.
I stole time and stole utopia.
I met some lovely people when I did that.
I was teaching poetry.
I visited friends and felt there was an unabashed fondness
even while preparing lunch.
When I came back, I knew my purpose was not a sunken pincushion.
I had some real clutch of consequence. I loved my lover better.

ON REBELLION

It was not a romantic sentiment, nor self-determined; rather, it was embarrassing.
My love of spearheading, from introvert to extrovert,
from cowardice to consequence, from the enjambment to the unspecified dunce.
It was a sabotage, a reckless moment: a purulent, tawny decree.
All temptation puzzled me and drew me in.
I dropped out of a large life,
I flew over exams, I punched out breakfast teachers with lunch money,
toiling over the idea of belonging rather than over upward mobility.
I understood how power flung outward
into the troves of the cursed (I felt cursed or troubled all of the time).
I wasn't bearing oranges, limes, or even lemons.
All of it blurred together so that a mere suggestion made by
an outside force was something to be freely ignored.
I could nod off, I could misinterpret, it could be reconfigured as a negotiation.
The fog felt like an aphorism. Never lifting, always dull,
always an added pull. The tribunal cloud judged below, judged my direction.
There was lying, conning, faking, elucidating in order to get away with undoing.
I was interested in preserving yet I can't tell you if it felt
sacred or befallen.

Your anxiety might have represented a crushing faith
or a character assassination, my own or someone else's.
Or a lack of grip on reality: the wet rip of the grocery bags
all of it falling—
your body on all fours.
Accumulating soot upon retrieval.

There were downsides to feeling different so I huddled
in the corner (not a ball, not rocking). I felt friendless and yet social.
I felt no aptitude towards refining a skill.
However, words cut my brain into two brains with their precipice
their demarcations, their incisions (too strong a word).

They held me captive against their edge,
their influence: I felt like insinuating something delicate or dear.

Now—I am holding on—trying to pay attention to the collusion that I must
be playing over and over in my mind, and it was my mind,
it needed me to leave everything outside, on the steps or in the sky,
to feign exhaustion in order to meet an aberration,
the one in the corner that felt large and carefree with its
own vernacular sprawled with whitewash on bricks or floors or that ghastly
far above that kept me standing very still but perhaps I wasn't inactive,
I was just interpreting what had already been an assumed boundary,
immersed in its insularity and in what stuck to its roundedness.

for KATY LEDERER

A LONG MATING SEASON

Popular novels never have original names, dates, or places
except for science fiction which never has original dates.

So futuristic that it turns itself on itself.
The scene in the final battle bemuses me
it seeks deductive models and modes.

A human body is in front of you.
The battering has left you withholding
all desire in the world from me.
A bell tower has found me;
an affectionate existentialist hanging on to the ropes

a secular humanist, a kind variant without a church.

Next, I pull down that lonely flag.
Why was it waving to you?
I really asked it to settle down to modest heights
which was difficult.
Mental distress taught me a thing or two.

Not moving rapidly, I stepped into the historic house
not to return, the forest hid the springwater pool,
I heard the Indigo Bunting lodged a spirit inside her
at the sight of him,
no star in view;

And you have not ever earned such rare and gifted colors.

I sighed: remarkable, a card shark would never signify
 such a creature yet a peddler would.

BLOWING HOT AND COLD

What does it mean to say that faith alone works?
Or that faith in itself can drag a whole mountain to the other side.
Of course faith rests its laurels on the impossibility of the fleet
of dreadfuls worshipping a magnetic bounty of light in
the neutral distance. I am tired of so much confusion,
of dreary, ugly ideas, of nonsense.
Now to strangers and friends—of columns of stars organized for the
     onlookers here,
any several of the tropical trees, any several hocus-pocus earth-
muffin types. You should just stay clueless amongst your granola
huts and your failed relationships. I was told everything
does go back to one's miserable family, and it's true it's
the root of all odes to neurosis. Look here
between the cherry, the sugar maple, and the shagbark hickory
you stand out like a sore thumb in Bethlehem. Accept that nature
itself wouldn't have you and your former sport of death of life
of foul-mouthed abuse, it is all egregious and against clairvoyance,
charitable dreams groomed for a billion swine.

INNER WEATHER

A purchase of futures was at the edge of all of this.
That trailing call, a cry; so as if to beckon the generosity
of a single soup kitchen or the stranger with the benign encroachment. Why
does it trouble me to stand over there. Why do I feel that I am over there? A
fountain addresses the lack. We wait for it to spurt; I wait for the dream-house
    to collapse.
That has to happen to vainglorious architecture.
Because it triggers more of those kind of feelings.
When can I expect the cloud to encase all of it, moving towards
its own recognizable base. Did it lead me? Did I follow that rumble?
Do I earn my keep? In a serious, meaningful way?
Do I know how to stretch reason away from accountability?
Are you inside this moment with me? I had wished it so but couldn't recollect
a time when anyone was. We all looked up and caught a sense
of it as it almost coughed or sneezed, but it was inanimate. It, too, was distant,
having taken leave succinct and strange though
cavernous, so wide inside.

INAUSPICIOUS BANQUETS

Fathom I can't of leaving you.
Must I this time,
learning with feeble lessons,
it was bad all those other times,
which were plainly other times.
I am not sure what I have in my hand:

A hatchet, a club, or a long-winded sentiment.

I am overly prepared yet utterly irresponsible.
To recite to you a lyric: O cherry blossom
and O are you a male concubine?
I like that image. Or the narrative:
The tiger was stuck up a Banyan tree
and glanced knowingly at me while you
visited me last afternoon.

I announced gleefully to him to flee
so that I could have a boarder.
I said I am two steps ahead of you mister!

I write a lengthy essay on enormity
in popular culture, in art and in big business,
how it can crush me into bits how everything can.

Let me let go of you
so you can be famous, strong, and wondrous
without any stumbling around.

To your highest of
elevations.

Since I fail to perceive most of the show
I only place bets from the headquarters, sight unseen.

FINITUDE

The quality of finitude is that it is diminished,
the lackluster buffeted
ask the plaintive for her hands in the matter and she will shrug.
Coverage left the front page to nothing new,
just a medical condition estranged from its causes and its diagnosis.
This is the trouble
with intention it's hollow. It's
personal too, it commemorates
itself—the self is finitude and the self is getting popular, drafted,
like architects who design funeral lamps more becoming than the last batch.

FOOL

I sat here for a long time and dreamt
that all the narrow platforms or the studies
in human species were enlightening
but we all miss the wherewithal of
wreaking pure havoc on the displacement
of focused lives. I wanted to stay a child
until I wanted desperately to be an adult;
in both cases, I wanted to be fun-loving.
Hey chickpea, where was that place we all
went to for Chinese food? When can I be
informal and alluring and adaptable
for consumption as well as a tropical
American for you to hold back.

SMALL-MOUTH FORTITUDE

To tell stories of the most saturated,
the impulse to ladle soup,
only a copper pot has its own personality
to a person. When you talk of misery locatable
in natural disasters I think the fear must
be revised to its tiny birth, every
land with a grand valley ridge, a puckered texture

not towards the development of the soluble self,
of the bodies
or persons in the morgue.
What of the indefinite comforts to and fro
what of goodness, in the habituation
of habitat, a province or district or
rye, horsetail, buckwheat, unmowed or unmoved.
Grass from the immigrant's flapping-bird wings

I am too notational fixing the characters
so they tattle to an interesting newcomer.
I can't afford to live
as the wretched doormat.
Yet I am no civil assigned good-doer—
a flexible definition is my impulse
what of reading and writing about an emulation
of what will only be Carter liberalism, you end up
only liberating the car-pool lane and what
of poems in the night what does translation
translate? The natural strain does land one in
the hedonism making shells, oyster white,
yet there is trouble in all the questions.

Who is saving the dime bag, and who is lifting
the market streets up by ill hands for inspection.

THE ANCIENT NAME

The black henna comes from Yemen
and the gilded girl made a run
for cover—the end of classical civilization,

the beginning of casual caregiving.
An organic chemistry,
an invented element,
closely implicating
fingerprint and sovereign,
entitling us to share a night together.
Making up my bed I will sew
a duvet from the lumberyard.
It was framed in terms of saucy hedging
or flirting for the causes.

DAME'S ROCKET

What a brittle time in my sense of history.
 I cannot wish for anything and cannot drop out of anything.
The proper or well-oiled can qualify
for the whole pot with one fell swoop,
but I, on the other hand, am a large destructive fire.

We crashed and burned, so what now?
Take me and carry me to the other place,
singe me with the complete honesty
of a jailbird, let's celebrate our singular
tribal victories, alone and lopsided.

SWAYBACK

A magnificent game called surplus
to chase the suitor with his or her own pants.
Thank you for coming to my party.
Thank you for your company.
Women are left on the prairie.
We, who are not amazons or feminine tycoons.
For a positive, plutonic, rendering
a different kind of assistance,
nothing you need your whole body for,
chores or noisemakers.

So let's not dig together for the layer of earth
beneath the surface, no let's not dig there.
Remember, I can get carried away.
And, we can't have too many cerebral and sexual convulsions,
we can try carrying all of our clothing away in roughed up bundles.
We could shove everything into the sack—
 a strong, wicked compulsion.

HERE AND HERE

A problem to be drenched
in troubles, window drawn
a sophist and an underachiever
sink into the puddle, never to return.

The little position
a deep pastoral,
green lamps and floor-bound
beds strike me
in all the wrong places.
Where did my urgency lead me?
From my heart to my head
to the blanched feet: all regional,

I sputtered—to flee or to grace
the problem with a masculine name so that
it becomes divisive and complimentary?

THE FLOWERS

I was cheered

        when I came first to know

that there were flowers also

    in hell.

        —William Carlos Williams

What awkward lines of passage
drawn like fabric over a century.
So my love's a distant cause
and patience is a virtue.
An opera is what to study first
then perhaps the novel,
when in fact, what came before
drew me to a poem. So decorative!
So scribbled—everything little flowers even.

THE CLOUD

In Brooklyn I crashed into the tree trying to be beautiful,
it was a funny (I was cradling my little discomfort).
I wanted what everyone seems
to want in Brooklyn, New York.
But where are the nerds that I think I can fall in love with?
I flit around to a tune as a kind of collusion with fear,
with a bony outer covering.
Your loose curls frame your hairline,
a line of the sky directing it all outward.
It was such a glorious memory.

Recently, I found a Moorish ivory casket that I was
okay with, a cat whisker was sharp enough to open
me up, a test of my deus ex machina.

TROUBLESOME

But now that I've walked around, it feels so hopeful.
You there, me here.
I am going to be thematic—
Working with a grandiose possibility
In order to keep my
values in place.
To forge a wanderlust,
Engross a subject to death.
Liable for the land of Nod—
So the land of isthmus—
Hydra not finally slain—
my gawky foot on a hinge,
I peruse my friends
to see what their rotary bags hold.
And I still remain difficult when it is advantageous.

THE SILENT MEOW

Under the parts of the Brooklyn Bridge, I was with Hedi and Angus.
We were discussing his cat's mute mewing.
Hedi and I perked up: What a metaphor for a woman we said.

This was a little off the cuff, because we are off the cuff
And were not that kind of feminist—
not to make such a drab and pathetic metaphor
likening a woman to a cat.
But we liked the persistence that the mute cat exhibited,
Its mewing, demonstrative yawns with nothing coming out—

it was the kind of perfect caption we had for such obvious things
and obvious needs for day-to-day living.

AFTER THE WEEKEND WITH GENIUSES

After the weekend with fiction writers full of pages,
I decide that a poet is a voyeur out to steal the reckonings or outcomes
of other people's lives, with shorthand; we grip with an ode
like a hoe, but not really to garden.

We are false gardeners who bask in the hot sun
seeking gentle cherubs to serve us lemonade,

we ache without the work but are extravagantly
candid; so much so, we fool ourselves into
staying poets. Living firmly on the lawn, outstretched like
Cupid, so that the vision stays comely, inviting.

for HEATHER MCGOWAN

LUCKY

What's come back
is the fruition—
a giddiness of
corrected vision.
A rarified history
majestic thoughts
fawns drunk

This way so much better.
Comedy from music.
It's this way nearby
when traveling issues
recollections of formative years or formative yearns.
Look the water ripples.
The grass is jointly
lush persisting in search of its decoration.

POET STATE

Why was it all drawn in with difficult laces?
My hands were bloody and I escaped through back doors
like they were front ones.
However, the plan, originally

was to not get this clever.
At least not now;
distant islands, distant pleasures.
Walk here and guide me in an instantaneous fall:
wicked, broken, centipedes and all that.
Gross daffodils, bold and shaped finely for pottery
so much like money, staying up late to shower
to cram frontiers in a base evolution
of hands, eyeballs,
damp cold feet.
An awkward dance, realized, how
balmy, how clammy.
Life: We've gotten it to be equitable,

and how not lucrative lucrative seems to be without sun.

YIELDING

In folklore this would be a lot of fun:
A reforesting or rebirth appropriate
to a natural heroism.

In New York or in the 21st Century
this makes me more of an animal—
a distressed one due to my inefficiencies.

Rejoicing in my bleak and well-mannered
submission, I actually can carry you along
twelve times on my back before I am weary.

Kindling and other material you manage
in with bravado is only the exterior of what I do.
I think there are neologisms for this now,
and it is not a trifling observation. It took

so many cultural propositions. Now weigh
them in front of me, tell me they are
worth looking into.

AMERICAN ARTIST

You're a nihilist engulfed in gabardine, hair strewn wild in the victim's
hood. Where are you really kept? Neither down here nor in heaven's pantoum.

Just divulge that everything has taken your hand or is immersed in
your beckoning. Your Midas touch sorrows, on lamps & on bellies.

Drop—let there be a drop, and push to be lifted again. You have no
dialectical will. The drowned self shut her eyes and never breathed again. What was

once ownership of a grand theme: walked into the room, onto the stage,
with the sexuality of a Grecian with the dank blank inside terror.

I wanted to ask but never dared—whom do you take orders from? Has
the body divided from the spirit? Are they in contest? In concert?

To remake mania into some placid sparing of responsibility—
without parable, remnant, or excess to challenge any abysmal raft.

OFF-YEAR: SEVERAL HOPES & HEALTH GAMES

1. Hopes of the Womenfolk

I am fond firstly of using maxims.
So firstly I must tell you one or two things.
Three or more are most likely to occur.

And if you were here, if you could see clearly
what was your American trait: your cocksure pleasantries
against my proposal of Euphoria. But ho hum.
I am fond of too many things. So there.

I am in a thatched Tudor, on a spiked road,
overlooking madness.
I am not in that madness.
So hunted I am or like to imagine that I am hunted.
My Euphoria. And thank you or forgive me.
And so haunted from the run-downness,
so dilapidated from boring mistrust residual of something
unlike any loyal animal.
You are not really a master!
I just invented this to control my own longings
or from separateness but I lick a wound
and find only secrecy. So there I was duplicitous.
I was attracted to the idea of self-expression.
There were blueberries.
There isn't anything left.
There is a dictionary of danger, the ways of communicating
forceful and striking: find it, dream it, resist it.
And I am here amongst the villages that black out.
From time to time, whistling creeps me out.
What songfest are you looking for?
I found the vintner very sexy. I found that I want to hold painters.
I found myself dusting ferns in quiet woods. Everything distilled,

everything vermilion. There are isolated instances of small game birds.
And a wasp with a vicious sting. A workhorse with a proper ethic,
and me bestselling to the air.
And car mania and street mania and sexual mania.
And the illustrious wood to tie oneself to.
We women get religion, so sadly, I will stop to cry.
And the mournful wing flips over on its ridge, translucent,
she to the trick, she tricks with no love behind it, now, dismantled,
using the maxim to clean her house, dropped it. Oh sad, spilled
to helpless activity and marked *as is, as is.*

2. Castanets and Her In-Between

Furnish a ringing and clickety-click
here, another ring one,
a present, callow. I am just
a provincial twit. I carried too generous a thing.
Spell my designs out and over-prepared
to say the least. Are they spells?
Thoughts echoic down to the base?
Killed as in an architectural click
like the brain as in synthesis, as before,
before it was a terminal thing bent out,
unable to sup a steel cup
but I started to sputter for nourishment.
I was trying to keep it all together, you might say,
         clipped or spanked hour of hysteria
have no tail. Typical.

Instead of a trance or what was perceived, I sprouted an architect's wing
and swept up the playground with a broom of tender desires.
The problem, oh say it was no problem: I had no grown-up in sight.
So I clicked or I got spanked.
Or the printed etiquette was that there were only performances.
The too-numerous-to-be-counted sat puritanical.

I dreamt about you last night, between the wrists, between
clasping the ring and the ringing focused on the floorboards.
I was held up in a cottage, I had a benefactor or a male friend for gullible glee.
You do not possess that kind of glee.
I am mitigated by a pushover's sleeve.
I've learned that you are no pushover.
I have taken also the hat of an architect. Oh, I miss some romance, learned
I'm not so much nice as distracted by what produces escapes
          that pass off sweetly as independence
or a trip to the midwife or desire in need of a translation.
I do love nobody. That clicking, some clanking nearby,
but no horses sped through. I was left. But somewhere nearby,
ringing, the trample-back-for, no, I am not really here,
here is my heart. I have another one and another one.
Is it that I believe the tips on the horses or the formal
speech of a caregiver? My veil covers the shadow's bank,
it's so bleak.

A FALLACY PETAL

Handwritten for a talking book, a sea-horse-flower.
Vaporous and then it disappears. Beckon, regret, skittish.
Such ticklish pages. And so the spirit of intention
is what haunts me and it is ugly.

I am not a child in that sense,
treason from proclivity.
Wonder underestimates the cliff.
That darling feeling was yesterday.
It was serenely devilish until it was wretched.
Tidings to the victuals and then where it goes.
Tidings to the viscera and the trickster's intestine.

Outnumbered, I sprang for the official's papers,
raised with doves, violets, and Bengal tigers,
and true notions of sacrifice. This was all so becoming in a way.
A novice in the care or protection of wild, maltreated animals,
loving indiscriminately. What season was it?

I never think one should discriminate, provided that walking
sticks are beating limbs. Like those policemen.
The lotus flower had no time in the lake with the lady.
The Fire next time is provident and gargantuan. No more vulgar
Latin. No mere terrorism, the larger the more engrossing,
the more fundamental.

VIEWPOINT

The life of a talking book,
of a sad sentence unable to declare
modern love for a somnambulist.
An apparently superhuman man will reveal nothing.
That grin you gave me showing your teeth quietly
will keep me sheltered here for more days than I had
imagined. Our paths will cross and it will be provisional.

BELONGING AS CONSEQUENCE: ON POETRY

It was just a momentary untruth in my way,
bodies of the crowd blocked the big blue outside.

Now I have a stealthy cause: to try and be myself,
to further a personal idea of arrangement,

of how to use those thoughts, the ones that don't get used.
But how to let them tick without abuse.

How to repay the debt, use the solvent,
blast the botched & troubled nearby—

What does everyone else caress?
All those etched poses neatly joined:

Mastery, hierarchy, witchcraft & shamanism.
A spike in the dander keeps me plain enough—

but to insist! To consolidate those fears—after months of uncertainty
couldn't cough or breathe or pilfer correctly.

Now this victorious shape, this idea moves
through muteness, shyness, weakness—

then it awakens:
Becomes a nonconformist happenstance—
A person saddled beneath

Reaches up for a fiction,
abundant and unrestricted ideas

poised and in front.

THE LONG WINTER

Her wooden nickels paid for wilderness
but had sprightly foes and merciless
confidantes. Everything is long and built
on sad occasions. Take a midwife and buy
her an ice-cold vodka with ginger beer.
Lose the meaning of a loss.
When is waywardness helpful
except as a chance to drink
the gleam of historical
promises—from literary greats
to transitional banquets
of hope driving the cattle home.

White hoofs and paths of sentimentality
jaunts with goats and crows
picked up the burden, and claimed
this could be animal life, this could
be a well-formed hesitance.
May we embrace the pause and herald it
as a gesture less towards mere wanderlust
and more the posture of the life of the mind's winding down
to its realistic urges.

BIRD AND NESTS

I got it you see. This time, O little drifting cardinal
I got the career along with a jeer
and a carelessness in my demeanor.
Careening purposefully,
I suppose, it was the only way
to get past you so you wouldn't see me.
Thus the night fled.
I had a central theme or concern that was chiefly
tender. Check lists for a stint upon the childish raft,
you laughed and called it pathetic.
For if I fell off I wouldn't know how to swim
and if I brandished a little Jeep Cherokee
and didn't know how to drive, I'd be both
a helpless woman and a rich one.

II. be my foreground

TRAVEL

I am traveling around this time with a group of listeners
fabricating little urchins. My mind is at unrest
for I am a drawstring tying up sex and heat.
A solid equidistance of rapture and mistakes scares me into
this place of bleating a sheep out of its discourse.
When I glanced at Spinoza, I felt the fear of ethics placating
me at this certain moment of defeat. Please, dearest of dear friends
draw me a map away from the pivotal moment when I surrender
my dignity to hedonism. No dropkick, no head-on into the blindness.
Billowing, hovering wind, I see you grab the trees and shake them.

HEREDITARY CURSE

I have to begin to send myself out there in some capacity.
Cramp the drift of the community-spirited into a minor time.
Mopping the floor may flatten my grip today but
increases my chances for less psychological floundering.
An undershirt, a moldy morning of duress and courtesy.
I have taken on a lover and have met suitors in various
workstations. I live in the pulse of art-making and capital.
I drink probably a little too much every other week.
Simply put, I am aware that I have established a
tender community of mindful people and drunks.
Amazed at this, actually.
There are two sets of flowers;
of their blue color and their yellow color.
Oh, how every man relates to the natural world differently
and to women the same, so we have not been compared,
there is no real dichotomy. that behavior rests in,
just theory for talk, acting out for action.
Climbing the stairs with groceries slung over the middle
of the arm and I hobble very quickly.

for RUTH MARGRAFF

SOURING RUSH

So the look of anger built an old Norse legend
of the Viking who jumped ship in the dragon's teeth
and the lemming's underbelly was a variant cause.
Classify the stars in your free time for
what else can you store for your cycle.
A fighting fish is more masculine than masculine
and more strangely human than a sailor.

BIRTHDAY POEM

When that boat soars off, my lover is full of
magnetic sensibilities, but there are French chemists
who've made pills for this. I tell my lover of just one week that
there are museums drunk with people.
Headrushes are lovely when cured,
as one cups an illustration of the densely crowded man who is my lover.
My lover is strangely seductive and punishing,
I can tell. On his birthday, I wish him a Happy Birthday
but I think he has a complicated head, it seems to frustrate
him. For I have seen him swoon and
has he spun around a bit too quick? And this may not be him.
My lover of one week swims with small finned fish and cypress
in the shape of oceans. And yes, I am in a stranger ocean
than I fished and my lover is just beside, with a possible foil,
curing me for a moment of all possible intricate characterizations.

after BILL LUOMA & BARBARA GUEST

ARABESQUE

Halfway up the mountain, there was an unforeseeable
Adonis in a bar with green floral detail in his eyes.

He was all skin and paraffin, tinted majolica.
A casual display, really. A ceremony of faith without

religion as is a bird chirping in a dead branch.
A drive with a most sound decadence,

and struck like a matchbook struck churns gleeful
personal belonging into a rambling Mustang GT.

Chalked up to forgery is charm,
make Mercury confess, and peach,

such that a law disposed to a strident tranquility
wills a clean white undershirted body

darning sporadic colors, a pinion of this lark, of a dear lark.

FREE OF WORRIES AND RESPONSIBILITIES

A monster is not your owner or keeper, and that it will never
love you is true in so many senses.
A ghostwriter understands when the truth doesn't apply.
And that you're spineless after much breaking down of heaving life
into hammers and shores of indifference, not spineless already,
not spineless in bed without a lick of concern for the aftermath.
Oh, to dismantle emotion and blanch it over the pool's ugly water—
no shimmer, just the possible shield of terror of too much.
And the arms and the joints ache like everyday, and we have that death.
Cufflinks and man-armor and handsome man charms.
And man from the beginning: a figure of torchlights and the knife,
I know it's true, it is all out there to be had as an arcane pact of truce and devastation,
for my twin life came for me and reared a difficult child head.
She said: Forget that desire is with error,
it is in a long corridor unbeknownst in its undress.

A BRAZEN STATE

If I remember that there was a course of action,
like a town with blueprints for the carnival,
then I can bludgeon my dream with an autocrat's
swiftness and catalogue all the experiences like sentences.
There was the one with a bald spot and the one getting one.
There was one with only a fawn for a friend and one
with a rifle. There was one with just a penny and twelve
zeros with fanaticism for nothing special.
What was edited came true, what was omitted was
lucky to be erased. There lies the town: the state's little anarchy
in trouble with hazy aqua for a light—a duress unbound in the children's play.
I forgot that it meant we were all brazen and strong-willed
and did not fight indiscriminately for terror or the experts.

after ADAM PHILLIPS

SEPTEMBER MY LOVER WEARS SWEATERS

My lover has a long, saber-shaped tail, is marked with a powerful beak.
He is also the fourth largest island called "The Town."
My lover protects soldiers by calling out their enemy's name
with an even keel even if it makes the women cry.
My lover has scratch marks on the back of his neck
and an itchy gray sweater that assumes his lovely green eyes.
He wears his only track record on his sleeve and tracks
down visions using Freudian analysis, he says "damn you,"
when he means, get out of my way. My lover is a chocolate
hangover with three kings, a messenger, and The Firm holding
up his velvet cape; there, they said, there you are.

FORGOTTEN VS. FORGETTING

The world is heavy
think of where   culture meets the complicity of cost
and   value, rickety from tide and moon.
It's fear and exaggeration   and often
Everyone is sent away fortified with sex.
Memory recollected only to feel major feelings.
Everyone wants to damn a consequence
that unequals this when said hurriedly,
o, this tugboat, o this tremble in my dress.

There are wayward hopes curing
the lack of history in our teeth,
it made everyone draw pictures of their long days,
of wrongness lingering, sour plates jilted
with bugs and fragments. And this was years.
I think it lasted with a somber disparate
trickery of gentle fields twisting behind brightness,
with important nobodies,
merely shade and daft starched fabric.

How to claim a real profession with a soft
spot for a veritable drop off the earth,
so that vulnerability can linger, a thousand times
I've thought to throttle this hope, after this,
I turned my face to a sky,
and imagined an isometric loss
for this direction of speech.

BE MY FOREGROUND

Travel from one place to another so that a day is old
and French words for sleep are cheerful and festive.
I worry that all the fun will kill me
like a good playing card, a dance card,
a dramatic card, a race card,
a baseball card, and a chairman's
grab at my linen underclothes.
For an intense lamp is not the sun.
A church, go there. Here is where faith lives.
A temple. Here is where devotion washes.
A sand dune is two bodies.
Made for the kitchen, made for drink,
made for the reader, made for life,
topological, having no outside, I fear
or inside, a province of smallness,
and how I cling to your end.
Here by a wreck of a road.

THE OTHER DALE
After Ashbery's "The Other Cindy"

The other Dale is an unnamed cat, different only in the way graphic
design is different. Different in the way a cat is always childless
but the other Dale is not. His ascendancy greatly modifies the loyal,
gentle fur on the most careful paws. What eastern horizon on the ledge
of simple astounding greatness, a silent perch facing the Brooklyn Bridge,
this other Dale writes novels in wayward meows, chooses parking
over the children playing: What similarities draw a man to a cat,
is it the kitten in a personality? This poem is laughable with mock seriousness
but the other Dale loves mock seriousness, which one is flying through the air
of appearances, both in a counterculture alley, hence making an imitation of
the other Dale, feigned but unpretended, with adoration brimming in coffee
cups or branches of the intelligence services lapping kitty milk
all over the corporation.

NEAR

He is a colorblind painter, a main character
a masculine in the Eleusinian mystery.
He is a simple head
declaring arcane knowledge
telling truths with a frayed sense.

He will rest from the NASCAR race
and matriculate a night vision into a day vision.

We will gallop to the circus to hock all of our relatives.
We validate the nearness of the loved
one who has risen and retreats.
Of the child who is led into mock-heroism.
And it is your little girl.

Our town is a middle imperial, a destitute town,
a restaurant row
longing for urban commerce
longing for towns to rule out emotions   in favor
of hardness of the sea and opaque lust.

The Soothsayer wants to tell him about settings:
            a tight path,   a bath, a sweetheart,   of love,
or that an obscure origin gallops nearest to him.
And that wouldn't be me
or the little girl.

With a sudden emphasis to get him to the station to the bedroom,
with a gallop again and the awkward appearance of sly requests
cleverly burning: wood piles near a sickbed.

He was central to the plot between the town and the country.
For he is with a daughter in the country.

The town, barely able to be law abiding
Quite frivolous as you will see.
Barely able to resist and can't dream.
He, a permanent diplomat, nursed the town
combining the composed parts.
                Favoring two equally desirable plots.
A heap of wood and a daughter's pyramid.

Lost the plot when he gave the little girl the Atlantic.

For AJA & DALE E. SHERRARD

EVERYWHERE

I must stammer now out of a growing happiness.
Behind the gowns of ferns,
the missing fortnights and robes of welcoming eyes
I plunked myself onto a cushiony mat.
Fetched the wellspring to a bounty.
I was crafting crafts, I had needles, I was sewing butterflies
like women do—but only in terms of thoughts,
not in terms of doing. Or I thought, alas,
lightness is part of the commune of despair.
I was daydreaming all sorts of conflictions.
But I must try: I mean to praise the dignity in everything.
The grandfather in a gentleman, the pool and glint of the yes.
O dearest, with underwear the color
of christenings, pure in fashion, doe-legs and pipe.
So I will be more discreet and you crass—it's okay.
Less the lady of candlelight, of deliberate pauses,
          but I was followed into the bedroom
with a talkative armchair
of green to the clandestine triumph—to the lovelorn,
towards a gymnasium of hopeful rows.
You are my beloved,
in more ways than one,
oblivion lifted into lavishness.   Can I wait?

Carousing a wrongful life into happiness.
For these first six months, after the last forgetful year,
this very night shone alone   in a clear fountain of,
 what should I call it?

Excitement. Brandishing high hopes,
Spirited solvent in pail
not wine nor food.

For the longest of times,
so not the light either.
Everywhere was like me,
I saw it clearer than ever,
I wasn't looking at a piece of art anymore, I was thinking now,
more succinctly, how to live in that danger, from error to infinite grasps
from my hand to the ledge to the golden dome cast from
giant ceilings
larger than life then why, yes,

certainly unearthly I had called it, but better
that I name it filthy
and am honest to all perversions of grandeur.
I asked you that which
I had hoped, to give your aberrations a place to sail far and in
sanctions less cavelike, since this was all talking into the late night.

SUBURBAN GHAZAL

A harbored thought folded into 300 honeybees. Muck from a rusted galleon
on the lawn, our little plot. This is how the story goes:

All of our chickens crossed the street and were killed
when the dog ran after them. Neighbors pulled their children in.

A leaf fluttered red downward. So into the cellar with a closet full of gross plastic
limbs, ugly toys. The woods hid the spying drecks from the bus stop
   where the story goes:

Thus the German Shepherd lunged at strangers, my chipped teeth, my babysitter's
plastic-wrapped broken toe. I erupted from out of the story.

This diversity. I cannot be treasonous, faltering to a crisp nobody on a neglected
street. I need to become somebody. So Jasmine dressed the foyer.

There were honest walks to commercial buildings, welcoming pivots' turnings, little
ancient blindfolds, tarnished garnet catches—caught in the car, my thumb.
   The story goes:

Winter allows every feeling to get into the house, backing a sick day up with tremors,
lest the dead grass brown everyone over and make us those *dirty* Indians.

SHOUTING

I asked an awkward boy to show me how I felt—
it was hell from the beginning.
I started to shout a tale about how trouble leans heavy:
What's the value in daydreaming about fortune
or, what's the daydream here?
Whittled down, for I've got trinkets
so gloomy and yet so everlasting.
Gems got me into this, as did cinema.
Give credence to stable thoughts outside in the anarchy.
Disarray is bare, it is the envy.
I jumped up to play house: Why?
Why can't I just stop shouting on.
One day, I got a job,
I got hitched, I got money,
I got busy with schedules
I got a broken telephone, a broken oven,
I felt that clean meant clean from
everything but reason.

Helpful it all was for making me private.
I understood how privacy came about in the flowers of the floor,
into the traverse, into a discourse where I yell at a friend about art-making;
not mine, someone else's.

What a sham privacy is, letting the pantry give you disasters, where you have
a mentality and a look at every turn, the cherubs,
the complacent cherubs—we turn away.

CONCENTRIC AND OUTWARD

One moves lightly over the grass;
not bestowed with a joyless drum
heavy at times so that a kite corners
the ground, air thins out into conversant tremble
akin to thinking.
Alas it feels like thinking; having wit

brings out genius in strangers,
Prospect Park, an angle of an incline.
Unearth several kinds of gratitude. Park rangers
sat on benches glittering at one time.

So softly kick dirt by a planter,
look up to kites for all that play—all that stealing towards the center.

for NINA D'AMARIO

ON IMMIGRATION

After being humiliated one continues the manuscript of identity.
Activities, diseases, doldrums, the crony affair after the situation,
the one where one faces how one is the undertaste,
how one isn't the neighbor, the piebaker, a white folk. How one isn't a gorgeous
dream wrapped up in tireless affection, primped for wider screens.
So there one grew, in the coffee sickness, the dictionary browsing
in a fury for the word entitlement to spill—

After convulsing with rage, one continues in the aftermath
of no friends on Tuesdays or shouting fiercely when nothing sobered
to the eleventh hour and the tide shrunk to its sense of privacy where it
had nothing to do with shores or moons, and humiliation sat on its lover's
knee, greeting the eccentric rich and the hourglass with such force
the rage enameled like fine paint to a sheen of deep blue.
Restless in the way that stirs the crowd to its feet to claim the encounter
for the intentions of personal gain without the empire, without the
embarrassment of shaking one's head, of resting it underneath the ground, to live
sanctioned in the migrancy with an ugly plate for the economy but working ever
so hard. So unplanned, so beyond what one did before the lack of dignity sang an
opera. And organized all the ideas, before rage shot a bird that had once watched
effortlessly all the comings and goings.

THINGS FOUND MUTE

      The format for an evening
(because there are so many)
      is bleak as mystics.
Stronger than ten bad mornings.
Stronger dormant screeches and a telephone directory
      Everything stumped into a problem.
Everything sent out to work,
the bulky, the grandeur,
totems drinking me under the table.
Carving footstools like Woodsmen.
      Sprawls lacking the freedom
      of energy   leave me in horror, I say.
Something is asunder in its laughable zone.
I may parent you over to my neck of the corner
and beg for everything that I won't
involve the morning with. Alas we drop
to drunk submission which I found
      abandoned and subdued,
ignored with its simplistic
stance wanting   nothing but forty winks.

AGAINST CAREER

For the poem in Providence
where something began,

While I was walking
around clean streets

White for no hesitant light withdrew.
It was all right
then and now.

I want to be there in Providence,
to bring all of the forethought

The earnest versus the habitual.
The scholar versus the drama student.
The poet versus the poet.
Love versus the erector set.
The drowning versus the disappearance.

Now back and the air is right, logically
New York City is both the future and the past,

I want to be a poet all of the time.

It's quiet enough for me to hear a siren's full call
And drunk laughing people not in the least bit cruel.

FICTION

It's an itchy modifier some mornings gearing up for the rarity,
tenacious glues shifting me to merriment from no steady interest.
A gazillion anxiety of hours.   A distrustful eye,
a cue to fall or not a cue, a nudge   or just encouragement.

And then the nothing again.   But what is sad is that
it all depends on my eyes to say yes instead of no,

with time to grieve, to obtain memories by swindles,
the cheat chains me here with no exceptional skill

at worrying the iron, oven, flood
or fire that will wreck an unsaved everything.

for JEFF ANDERSON

60

RELEASE ME FROM THIS PAYING PASSENGER

There is nothing to really note in this world
you might say. But since crescent moons
frame brittle grass all over the world,
I won't stop at this philosophy. I won
the argument yesterday when we were nearby
the park and the day before when you ran me over.
I have run away from you with accidental
fortune in hands not all of your bank statements.
But I am not a Calvinist in the true sense I only
lowered it to ahistorical terms. I believe in principles
prophetic principles. You say marred and I say martyr.
I drink two liters; you don't drink anything.
There are pests roaming the floorboards.
There are animals all around us now.
Save the foolhardy measure for your male companions.
They desire this more readily
more enigma, shall we say, to entertain them
barren matadors or empathetics.
I need neither Grand Marnier nor vodka
to wash my throat or collapse my senses to tiny
careless obliterations. The way this ended shut you out,
so drop the lensatic compass and lavish gift, and please, run.

BACKGROUND

Mind you, or mind the mind—
Did it occur to you—that it did so many things at once?
Its battle lies mostly in convincing us to feel good
That thinking is always a bit uncomfortable.
"I could be doing something," it said out loud.
Other people learn the truth. I forgot each time, each time I worried a bit more.
Other people mine the importance of, the value in, great books, good literature.
I, too, regard it highly—So high that I can't reach the shelf.
Yet, things come to me that can't be helped,
I read about the brain in the Sunday *New York Times,*
I read about writing from people I despise but then when I keep reading,
I can't help but find them romantic and see how they participated in a whole era,
they made history, they invited me into the landscape—
And I'm the recipient of everything they've done.
Perhaps there is fear in discovering a book:
There are many things that can happen
when the ideas are brought to the center
for a confrontation with several wants and desires listed.
I don't know if I am fighting my impulses to join them.

Fence Books is an extension of **FENCE**, a biannual journal of poetry, fiction, art, and criticism that has a mission to redefine the terms of accessibility by publishing challenging writing distinguished by idiosyncrasy and intelligence rather than by allegiance with camps, schools, or cliques. It is part of our press's mission to support writers who might otherwise have difficulty being recognized because their work doesn't answer to either the mainstream or to recognizable modes of experimentation.

The Motherwell Prize (formerly the Alberta Prize) is an annual series, generously endowed by Jennifer S. Epstein, which offers publication of a first or second book of poems by a woman, as well as a five thousand dollar cash prize.

Our second prize series is the Fence Modern Poets Series. This contest is open to poets of any gender and at any stage of career, and offers a one thousand dollar cash prize in addition to book publication.

For more information about either prize, visit www.fencebooks.com, or send an SASE to: Fence Books/[Name of Prize], New Library 320, University at Albany, 1400 Washington Avenue, Albany, NY, 12222.

For more about **FENCE**, visit www.fencemag.com.

FENCE BOOKS

THE ALBERTA PRIZE

The Cow	Ariana Reines
Practice, Restraint	Laura Sims
A Magic Book	Sasha Steensen
Sky Girl	Rosemary Griggs
The Real Moon of Poetry and Other Poems	Tina Brown Celona
Zirconia	Chelsey Minnis

FENCE MODERN POETS SERIES

Structure of the Embryonic Rat Brain	Christopher Janke
The Stupefying Flashbulbs	Daniel Brenner
Povel	Geraldine Kim
The Opening Question	Prageeta Sharma
Apprehend	Elizabeth Robinson
The Red Bird	Joyelle McSweeney

ANTHOLOGIES & CRITICAL WORKS

Not for Mothers Only: Contemporary Poets on Child-Getting & Child-Rearing
Catherine Wagner & Rebecca Wolff, editors

FREE CHOICE POETRY

Bad Bad	Chelsey Minnis
Snip Snip!	Tina Brown Celona
Yes, Master	Michael Earl Craig
Swallows	Martin Corless-Smith
Folding Ruler Star	Aaron Kunin
The Commandrine and Other Poems	Joyelle McSweeney
Macular Hole	Catherine Wagner
Nota	Martin Corless-Smith
Father of Noise	Anthony McCann
Can You Relax in My House	Michael Earl Craig
Miss America	Catherine Wagner

FREE CHOICE FICTION

Flet: A Novel	Joyelle McSweeney
The Mandarin	Aaron Kunin